[This is] a blessed Book which We have revealed to you, [O Muhammad], that they might reflect upon its verses and that those of understanding would be reminded.

[Quran 38:29]

How to use this journal:

Theme and Verse Number: Start with your choice of verse.

Arabic: Regardless of the level you are, practice Arabic writing by copying down the verse.

Translation: Write down the translation you best understand and connect with.

Tafsir: Read through and write the background, context, and explanation of each verse. The most well known authentic resource for tafsir is Tafsir Ibn Kathir. This can be purchased online or in many Islamic bookstores. Tafsir Ibn Kathir can also be found for free online in various places.

Application: Reflect on and apply the verse of the day to your life. How does this verse connect to you and your experiences? How does it relate to the overall theme? Are there any other verses, hadith, or quotes that this brings to mind? How does it make you feel? How can you act on it? These are some questions to get you started, but of course you can write whatever feels right.

Dua: Write a short dua to help you put your learnings about the verse into action.

Ameen. May Allah accept all your efforts in better connecting with the Quran.

Why is tafsir important?

As Muslims, we get reward just for reciting one letter of the Quran, and for those who have difficulty reciting but endeavor to do it anyway, there is even more reward.

The Quran is, first and foremost, revelation sent to us to teach us how to live our lives in this world. That end will never be achieved if we continue only reciting empty words in a language we don't understand. And while it is good to read the translation of the Quran if you are not an Arabic speaker, even that cannot give us the full picture of the beauty and scope of the Quran.

Reading about, studying, and learning tafsir is what allows us to actually implement the Quran in our daily lives.

In addition to explaining interpretations of verses, Tafsir gives us the background and context for when, why, and how that verse was revealed. Knowing the circumstances behind a verse can help us to understand how it applies to our lives as Muslims today.

Verses of the Quran are not meant to be taken in isolation. Tafsir helps us to connect the verse we are reading with the verses immediately around it and the surah as a whole. We can see the bigger picture this way, and how one theme flows into another, as well as the wisdom behind why this verse is placed where it is.

Tafsir also makes the connections between the verse we are reading and the Quran as a whole, as well as relevant hadith. This can help give us a deeper understanding of the general theme and its place in our deen.

Finally, and perhaps most importantly, tafsir shows us how each verse is meant to be acted upon and implemented in our daily lives.

Surah: Verse:

Arabic:

Translation:

Tafsir:

Application:

Dua:

Surah:

Verse:

Arabic:

Translation:

Tafsir:

Application:

Dua:

Surah: Verse:

Arabic:

Translation:

Tafsir:

Application:

Dua:

Surah: Verse:

Arabic:

Translation:

Tafsir:

Application:

Dua:

Surah: **Verse:**

Arabic:

Translation:

Tafsir:

Application:

Dua:

Surah:

Verse:

Arabic:

Translation:

Tafsir:

Application:

Dua:

Surah: **Verse:**

Arabic:

Translation:

Tafsir:

Application:

Dua:

Surah: Verse:

Arabic:

Translation:

Tafsir:

Application:

Dua:

Surah: Verse:

Arabic:

Translation:

Tafsir:

Application:

Dua:

Surah:

Verse:

Arabic:

Translation:

Tafsir:

Application:

Dua:

Surah: Verse:

Arabic:

Translation:

Tafsir:

Application:

Dua:

Surah: Verse:

Arabic:

Translation:

Tafsir:

Application:

Dua:

Surah:	Verse:

Arabic:

Translation:

Tafsir:

Application:

Dua:

Surah: Verse:

Arabic: Translation:

Tafsir:

Application:

Dua:

Surah: Verse:

Arabic:

Translation:

Tafsir:

Application:

Dua:

Surah: Verse:

Arabic:

Translation:

Tafsir:

Application:

Dua:

Surah: Verse:

Arabic:

Translation:

Tafsir:

Application:

Dua:

Surah: Verse:

Arabic:

Translation:

Tafsir:

Application:

Dua:

Surah: Verse:

Arabic: Translation:

Tafsir:

Application:

Dua:

Surah: Verse:

Arabic: Translation:

Tafsir:

Application:

Dua:

Surah: Verse:

Arabic: Translation:

Tafsir:

Application:

Dua:

Surah: Verse:

Arabic: **Translation:**

Tafsir:

Application:

Dua:

Surah: Verse:

Arabic:

Translation:

Tafsir:

Application:

Dua:

Surah: Verse:

Arabic: **Translation:**

Tafsir:

Application:

Dua:

Surah: Verse:

Arabic:

Translation:

Tafsir:

Application:

Dua:

Surah: Verse:

Arabic:

Translation:

Tafsir:

Application:

Dua:

Surah: Verse:

Arabic:

Translation:

Tafsir:

Application:

Dua:

Surah: Verse:

Arabic: Translation:

Tafsir:

Application:

Dua:

Surah: Verse:

Arabic:

Translation:

Tafsir:

Application:

Dua:

Surah:

Verse:

Arabic:

Translation:

Tafsir:

Application:

Dua:

Surah: Verse:

Arabic:

Translation:

Tafsir:

Application:

Dua:

Surah: Verse:

Arabic:

Translation:

Tafsir:

Application:

Dua:

Surah: Verse:

Arabic:

Translation:

Tafsir:

Application:

Dua:

Surah: Verse:

Arabic:

Translation:

Tafsir:

Application:

Dua:

Surah: *Verse:*

Arabic:

Translation:

Tafsir:

Application:

Dua:

Surah:

Verse:

Arabic:

Translation:

Tafsir:

Application:

Dua:

Surah: Verse:

Arabic:

Translation:

Tafsir:

Application:

Dua:

Surah: Verse:

Arabic: Translation:

Tafsir:

Application:

Dua:

Surah: *Verse:*

Arabic:

Translation:

Tafsir:

Application:

Dua:

Surah: Verse:

Arabic: Translation:

Tafsir:

Application:

Dua:

Surah: Verse:

Arabic:

Translation:

Tafsir:

Application:

Dua:

Surah: **Verse:**

Arabic:

Translation:

Tafsir:

Application:

Dua:

Surah:

Verse:

Arabic:

Translation:

Tafsir:

Application:

Dua:

Surah: Verse:

Arabic: Translation:

Tafsir:

Application:

Dua:

Surah: **Verse:**

Arabic:

Translation:

Tafsir:

Application:

Dua:

Surah:　　　　　　　　　　　Verse:

Arabic:　　　　　　　　　　　Translation:

Tafsir:

Application:

Dua:

Surah: Verse:

Arabic:

Translation:

Tafsir:

Application:

Dua:

Surah: Verse:

Arabic:

Translation:

Tafsir:

Application:

Dua:

Surah: Verse:

Arabic:

Translation:

Tafsir:

Application:

Dua:

Surah: Verse:

Arabic:

Translation:

Tafsir:

Application:

Dua:

Surah: Verse:

Arabic:

Translation:

Tafsir:

Application:

Dua:

Surah: **Verse:**

Arabic:

Translation:

Tafsir:

Application:

Dua:

Surah: **Verse:**

Arabic:

Translation:

Tafsir:

Application:

Dua:

Surah: Verse:

Arabic:

Translation:

Tafsir:

Application:

Dua:

Surah: Verse:

Arabic:

Translation:

Tafsir:

Application:

Dua:

Surah: **Verse:**

Arabic:

Translation:

Tafsir:

Application:

Dua:

Surah:　　　　　　　　　　Verse:

Arabic:

Translation:

Tafsir:

Application:

Dua:

Surah: Verse:

Arabic:

Translation:

Tafsir:

Application:

Dua:

Surah:

Verse:

Arabic:

Translation:

Tafsir:

Application:

Dua:

Surah: Verse:

Arabic:

Translation:

Tafsir:

Application:

Dua:

Surah:

Verse:

Arabic:

Translation:

Tafsir:

Application:

Dua:

Surah: Verse:

Arabic: Translation:

Tafsir:

Application:

Dua:

Surah: Verse:

Arabic:

Translation:

Tafsir:

Application:

Dua:

Surah: **Verse:**

Arabic:

Translation:

Tafsir:

Application:

Dua:

Surah: Verse:

Arabic:

Translation:

Tafsir:

Application:

Dua:

Surah: Verse:

Arabic:

Translation:

Tafsir:

Application:

Dua:

Surah: Verse:

Arabic:

Translation:

Tafsir:

Application:

Dua:

Surah: Verse:

Arabic: Translation:

Tafsir:

Application:

Dua:

Surah: Verse:

Arabic:

Translation:

Tafsir:

Application:

Dua:

Surah: Verse:

Arabic:

Translation:

Tafsir:

Application:

Dua:

Surah:

Verse:

Arabic:

Translation:

Tafsir:

Application:

Dua:

Surah: Verse:

Arabic: Translation:

Tafsir:

Application:

Dua:

Surah: Verse:

Arabic:

Translation:

Tafsir:

Application:

Dua:

Surah: Verse:

Arabic: Translation:

Tafsir:

Application:

Dua:

Surah: Verse:

Arabic:

Translation:

Tafsir:

Application:

Dua:

Surah: Verse:

Arabic:

Translation:

Tafsir:

Application:

Dua:

Surah: Verse:

Arabic:

Translation:

Tafsir:

Application:

Dua:

Surah: **Verse:**

Arabic:

Translation:

Tafsir:

Application:

Dua:

Surah: Verse:

Arabic:

Translation:

Tafsir:

Application:

Dua:

Surah: Verse:

Arabic:

Translation:

Tafsir:

Application:

Dua:

Surah: Verse:

Arabic:

Translation:

Tafsir:

Application:

Dua:

Surah: Verse:

Arabic:

Translation:

Tafsir:

Application:

Dua:

Surah: **Verse:**

Arabic:

Translation:

Tafsir:

Application:

Dua:

Surah: Verse:

Arabic:

Translation:

Tafsir:

Application:

Dua:

Surah: Verse:

Arabic:

Translation:

Tafsir:

Application:

Dua:

Surah: Verse:

Arabic:

Translation:

Tafsir:

Application:

Dua:

Surah: Verse:

Arabic:

Translation:

Tafsir:

Application:

Dua:

Surah: **Verse:**

Arabic:

Translation:

Tafsir:

Application:

Dua:

Surah: *Verse:*

Arabic:

Translation:

Tafsir:

Application:

Dua:

Surah: Verse:

Arabic:

Translation:

Tafsir:

Application:

Dua:

Surah: **Verse:**

Arabic:

Translation:

Tafsir:

Application:

Dua:

Surah: Verse:

Arabic: Translation:

Tafsir:

Application:

Dua:

Surah: Verse:

Arabic:

Translation:

Tafsir:

Application:

Dua:

Surah: **Verse:**

Arabic:

Translation:

Tafsir:

Application:

Dua:

Surah: Verse:

Arabic:

Translation:

Tafsir:

Application:

Dua:

Surah: Verse:

Arabic:

Translation:

Tafsir:

Application:

Dua:

Surah: Verse:

Arabic:

Translation:

Tafsir:

Application:

Dua:

Surah: Verse:

Arabic: Translation:

Tafsir:

Application:

Dua:

Surah: Verse:

Arabic:

Translation:

Tafsir:

Application:

Dua:

Surah: Verse:

Arabic:

Translation:

Tafsir:

Application:

Dua:

Surah: Verse:

Arabic:

Translation:

Tafsir:

Application:

Dua:

Surah: Verse:

Arabic:

Translation:

Tafsir:

Application:

Dua:

Surah: Verse:

Arabic:

Translation:

Tafsir:

Application:

Dua:

Surah: Verse:

Arabic:

Translation:

Tafsir:

Application:

Dua:

Surah: Verse:

Arabic:

Translation:

Tafsir:

Application:

Dua:

Surah: Verse:

Arabic:

Translation:

Tafsir:

Application:

Dua:

Surah: Verse:

Arabic:

Translation:

Tafsir:

Application:

Dua:

Surah: Verse:

Arabic:

Translation:

Tafsir:

Application:

Dua:

Surah: Verse:

Arabic:

Translation:

Tafsir:

Application:

Dua:

Surah: Verse:

Arabic:

Translation:

Tafsir:

Application:

Dua:

Surah: **Verse:**

Arabic:

Translation:

Tafsir:

Application:

Dua:

Surah: Verse:

Arabic:

Translation:

Tafsir:

Application:

Dua:

Surah: Verse:

Arabic: Translation:

Tafsir:

Application:

Dua:

Surah: Verse:

Arabic:

Translation:

Tafsir:

Application:

Dua:

Surah: Verse:

Arabic:

Translation:

Tafsir:

Application:

Dua:

Surah: Verse:

Arabic: Translation:

Tafsir:

Application:

Dua:

Surah: Verse:

Arabic:

Translation:

Tafsir:

Application:

Dua:

Surah:

Verse:

Arabic:

Translation:

Tafsir:

Application:

Dua:

Surah: Verse:

Arabic:

Translation:

Tafsir:

Application:

Dua:

Surah: Verse:

Arabic:

Translation:

Tafsir:

Application:

Dua:

Surah: Verse:

Arabic:

Translation:

Tafsir:

Application:

Dua:

Surah: Verse:

Arabic:

Translation:

Tafsir:

Application:

Dua:

Surah: Verse:

Arabic:

Translation:

Tafsir:

Application:

Dua:

Surah: Verse:

Arabic: Translation:

Tafsir:

Application:

Dua:

Surah: Verse:

Arabic:

Translation:

Tafsir:

Application:

Dua:

Surah: Verse:

Arabic:

Translation:

Tafsir:

Application:

Dua:

Surah: Verse:

Arabic:

Translation:

Tafsir:

Application:

Dua:

Surah:	Verse:

Arabic:	Translation:

Tafsir:

Application:

Dua:

Surah: Verse:

Arabic: Translation:

Tafsir:

Application:

Dua:

Surah: Verse:

Arabic:

Translation:

Tafsir:

Application:

Dua:

Surah: **Verse:**

Arabic:

Translation:

Tafsir:

Application:

Dua:

Surah: Verse:

Arabic:

Translation:

Tafsir:

Application:

Dua:

Surah: Verse:

Arabic:

Translation:

Tafsir:

Application:

Dua:

Surah: Verse:

Arabic:

Translation:

Tafsir:

Application:

Dua:

Surah: Verse:

Arabic:

Translation:

Tafsir:

Application:

Dua:

Surah: Verse:

Arabic: Translation:

Tafsir:

Application:

Dua:

Surah:

Verse:

Arabic:

Translation:

Tafsir:

Application:

Dua:

Surah: Verse:

Arabic:

Translation:

Tafsir:

Application:

Dua:

Surah: **Verse:**

Arabic:

Translation:

Tafsir:

Application:

Dua:

Surah: **Verse:**

Arabic:

Translation:

Tafsir:

Application:

Dua:

Surah: Verse:

Arabic:

Translation:

Tafsir:

Application:

Dua:

Surah: **Verse:**

Arabic:

Translation:

Tafsir:

Application:

Dua:

Surah: Verse:

Arabic:

Translation:

Tafsir:

Application:

Dua:

Surah: Verse:

Arabic: Translation:

Tafsir:

Application:

Dua:

Surah: Verse:

Arabic:

Translation:

Tafsir:

Application:

Dua:

Surah: Verse:

Arabic:

Translation:

Tafsir:

Application:

Dua:

Surah: Verse:

Arabic:

Translation:

Tafsir:

Application:

Dua:

Surah: Verse:

Arabic:

Translation:

Tafsir:

Application:

Dua:

Surah: Verse:

Arabic:

Translation:

Tafsir:

Application:

Dua:

www.ingramcontent.com/pod-product-compliance
Lightning Source LLC
Chambersburg PA
CBHW081507080526
44589CB00017B/2676